Sing a Song of Christmas

written by Margaret Hillert

illustrated by Judy Hand

Copyright © 1989 by Margaret Hillert
Library of Congress Catalog Card No. 88-63571
Published by The STANDARD PUBLISHING Company, Cincinnati, Ohio
Division of STANDEX INTERNATIONAL Corporation. Printed in U.S.A.

HOW I KNOW

How do I know it's Christmastime?
How can I always tell?
Bells there are that suddenly chime,
Wonderful things to smell,
People and packages, secrets and song,
Holly wreath at the door,
Colored lights as we drive along,
Shoppers in every store.
Carols and cookies and candy canes,
Mysterious things to hide,
Snowflakes glowing through window panes,
And a lovely feeling inside.

WHEN CHRISTMAS COMES

When Christmas comes
God's creatures need
A helping hand
For gifts of seed,
Some nuts and apples,
Bread crumbs, too.
God's Christmas giver
Could be you.

CHRISTMAS CARD

God sent a Christmas card this year
For everyone to see:
A bright red cardinal tops the snow
At the tip of our evergreen tree.

SHEPHERD BOY

Shepherd boy, shepherd boy,
Tending to your sheep,
Did the angel's song of joy
Wake you from your sleep?
Do you know a baby lies
In the manger hay?
Hurry, hurry with your gift
For Him this Christmas day.

SINGING STARS

Christmas bells are ringing.
All the stars are singing.
Candles gleam with golden light
Welcoming the babe this night.

A KING IS BORN

Angel voices fill the air,
And all the stars are singing.
Gentle voices speak of peace.
Cathedral bells are ringing.
This is the wondrous news they bring.
This is the birthday of a king.

CHRISTMAS COOKIES

Cookie wreaths with bits of cherry.
Cookie angels frosted bright.
Cookie men with faces merry.
Cookie canes so sweet to bite.
Best of all the cookie star
Like wise men followed from afar.

CHRISTMAS TREE

We got into the car one day,
And then we drove a long, long way.
We walked into a little wood
To where a little pine tree stood.
We brought it home with us, and now
We're putting things upon each bough.
Oh, how surprised it's going to be
To turn into a Christmas tree.

TRIMMING THE TREE

We start with lights on branches bare,
And ornaments hung here and there.
Some silver rope goes looping through.
We add a silver bell or two,
And always, just before we stop,
A silver angel at the top.
Then in the softly colored glow
We set the manger scene below.

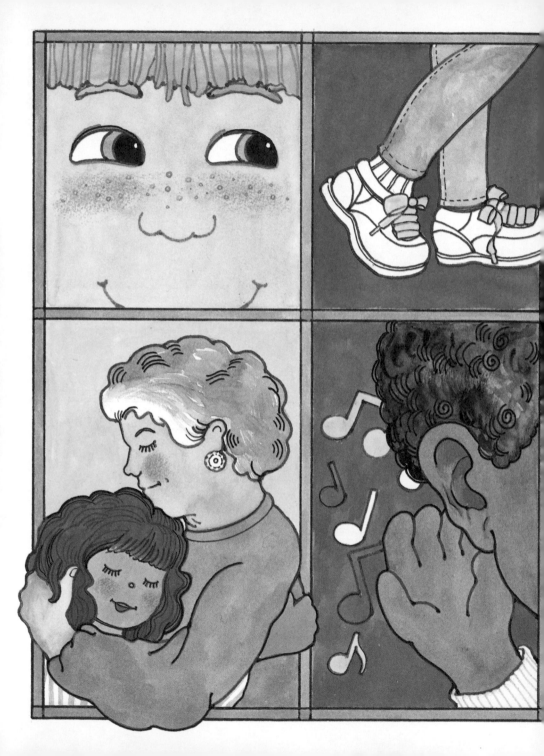

A CHRISTMAS THANK YOU

Thank You, Lord, for ears to hear
Christmas carols sweet and clear.
Thank You, too, for eyes to see
Colored lights on bush and tree.
Thanks for legs that run to meet
Friends and neighbors on the street.
Thanks for arms that hug and hold
As stories of the babe are told.
Most of all our thanks we bring
For Baby Jesus born a king.

CHRISTMAS DAY

Trees are bright
With colored light
And decorations gay.
Hearts are bright
With God's own light
And love on Christmas day.

CHRISTMAS GIFT

I looked and looked until I found
The nicest gift of all.
I tiptoed in without a sound
And hurried down the hall.
I wrapped it up and tied it well
And hid it on a shelf.
I'm so afraid that I might tell,
I'd better hide myself.

A CHRISTMAS LULLABY

Hushaby, rockaby, softly to sleep,
Soft as the snow that is drifting and blowing.
Hushaby, rockaby, shadows are deep
Blue on the snow that is endlessly snowing.
Sleep like the animals sleepily curled
In soft little nests in a winter white world.
Hushaby, rockaby, till the stars creep
Into a day that is shining and glowing.

SNOW ANGELS

When the snow is all around,
Flatten out against the ground.
Let your arms move to and fro
To make an angel in the snow.

CHRISTMAS MAIL

Mother gets mail.
And Daddy gets mail.
I never get anything—
Ever!
But today I got a card,
My very own card,
And I think that I'll keep it
Forever.

THE CHRISTMAS BABY

Two candles tall, and in between
We put the little manger scene:
A bright star hanging from a thread,
Mary bowing low her head,
Joseph standing straight and tall,
Shepherds kneeling near the stall
And when we put the baby in,
We feel the Christmas joy begin.

SING A SONG

Sing a song of Christmas,
Stars, and sleigh bells, too.
Sing a song of candy canes
And carols ever new.
Sing a song of angels
In choirs up above.
Sing a song of Christmas.
Sing a song of love.